A

SCIENCE IN
ANCIENT GREECE

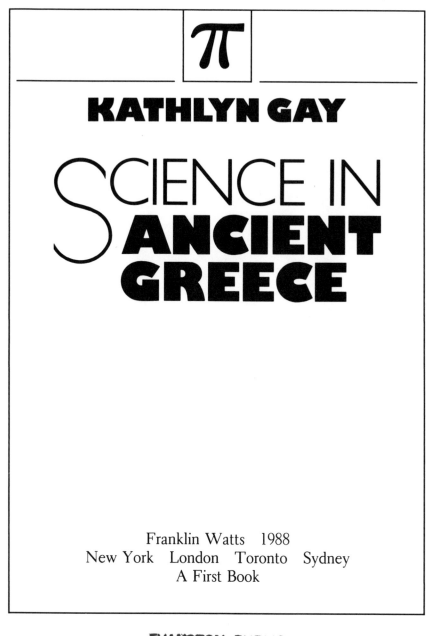

KATHLYN GAY

SCIENCE IN ANCIENT GREECE

Franklin Watts 1988
New York London Toronto Sydney
A First Book

Cover photograph by Ronald Sheridan/Ancient Art & Architecture Collection.

Photographs courtesy of: National Library of Medicine: pp. 8, 23; Hirmer Archive: p. 11; Ronald Sheridan/Ancient Art & Architecture Collection: pp. 19, 80, 83; New York Public Library Picture Collection: p. 27; Trustees of the Science Museum, London: p. 29; Burndy Library, Norwalk, CT: pp. 32, 66; From *A Popular History of Science* by Robert Routledge, London, 1859: p. 37; Smithsonian Institution/The Dibner Library: pp. 40, 47, 61, 75 (both); American Geographical Society (from Brumbaugh, *Ancient Greek Gadgets and Mechanics*): p. 45 (top); The Bettmann Archive, Inc.: p. 45 (bottom), 54, 59, 69, 72; The Granger Collection: pp. 51, 56.

Maps by Vantage Art, Inc.

Library of Congress Cataloging-in-Publication Data

Gay, Kathlyn.
Science in ancient Greece / Kathlyn Gay.
p.   cm.—(A First book)
Bibliography: p.
Includes index.
Summary: Discusses the theories of ancient Greek philosopher-scientists such as Ptolemy, Pythagoras, Hippocrates, and Aristotle, and describes scientific discoveries and their applications in ancient Greece.
ISBN 0-531-10487-7
1. Science—Greece—History—Juvenile literature. 2. Engineering—Greece—History—Juvenile literature. 3. Science, Ancient— Juvenile literature. 4. Scientists—Greece—Juvenile literature. 5. Engineers—Greece—Juvenile literature. 6. Philosophers—Greece—Juvenile literature. [1. Science—Greece —History. 2. Technology—Greece—History. 3. Scientists—Greece. 4. Philosophers—Greece.] I. Title.
Q127.G7G39   1988
509.38—dc19   87-23747   CIP   AC

CONTENTS

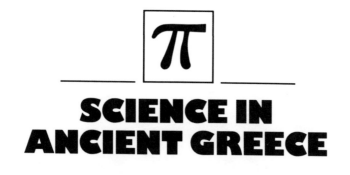

SCIENCE IN
ANCIENT GREECE

Thales of Miletus, the first known
important Greek scientist

1
PHILOSOPHERS OF NATURE

"Know thyself" is a saying heard today, but it is as old as Hellas, or ancient Greece. The man who first offered this bit of advice is said to be Thales (THAY leez), of the Greek colony of Miletus (my LEE tus). According to legend, Thales was one of Seven Wise Men whose ideas on politics and philosophy flourished among Greek-speaking peoples of the sixth century B.C. But Thales' name heads the list of sages. He is considered to be the world's first "physiologist," or philosopher of nature. He studied natural forces and formulated rational ideas about what the world is made of and how it works.

Before Thales' time, the laws of nature were thought to have been established by a variety of gods. Supernatural or mythical forces supposedly ruled people's lives and their natural environment. People made animal sacrifices as they asked the gods to bring about changes in everything from the weather to the outcome of wars.

No one can be sure why Greek science blossomed as it did in a culture dominated by beliefs that the gods had absolute power over people and nature. But historians believe that the seeds were planted long before Thales and other sages of the sixth century B.C. developed their ideas.

EARLY CIVILIZATIONS

The Minoans were an early people who greatly influenced the ancient Greeks. Between 3000 and about 1900 B.C., they built a sophisticated civilization on Crete, the largest island south of what is now the Greek mainland. Named after a legendary ruler, King Minos, the Minoans (my NO ahns) built huge palaces and other large structures; today they would be known as master architects and engineers. In addition, the Minoans paid special attention to their natural environment. They painted realistic pictures of plants, animals, birds, and fish on pottery and walls.

The ancient Greeks were also influenced by the Mycenaeans (my SEE nee ahns), who from around 1580 to 1100 B.C. occupied Crete and other islands in the Aegean Sea. The Mycenaeans—the first Greek-speaking people—developed a powerful culture, producing splendid buildings and mighty walled cities.

Both the Minoan and Mycenaean civilizations gave way to invaders and crumbled before natural disasters such as volcanic eruptions and earthquakes. A period called the "dark ages" followed, when wars between city-states for territory were commonplace. Each ancient Greek community was organized as a city-state with its own separate government. Each city-state and its surrounding countryside was an independent region ruled by a king, a group of wealthy families, or a dictator.

As city-states grew, some became overpopulated, so Greek-speaking people began to move into Italy and other regions of the Aegean (ee JEE un). Cities along the western coast of Asia Minor—now known as Turkey—were settled by the Ionians, a

Remains of a Minoan temple

ANCIENT GREECE
and other countries
~ 450 B.C.

BLACK SEA

ASIA MINOR

PERSIA

SYRIA

PHOENICIA

CYPRUS

• Troy
• Ephesus
• Miletus

Alexandria

EGYPT

CRETE

MACEDONIA

GREECE

PELOPONNESUS

Sparta •

MEDITERRANEAN SEA

ADRIATIC SEA

Croton •

Elea •

Rome •

SICILY

Syracuse •

ITALY

ANCIENT GREECE
~ 450 B.C.

ABDERA

AEGEAN
SEA

MACEDONIA

ASIA MINOR

SKIROS

LESBOS

CHIOS

•Thebes
•Athens

MYCENAE

• Ephesus
• Miletus

KEOS

SAMOS

PELOPONNESUS

SYROS

•Sparta

NAXOS

CNIUS

MELOS

MEDITERRANEAN SEA

CYTHERA

THERA

RHODES

CARPATHOS

CRETE

tribal group from mainland Greece. The area eventually became known as Ionia.

THE PAST PRESERVED

The Ionians did not build cities as magnificent as those of earlier cultures, but they carried on many of the building and metalworking techniques established by the Minoans and Mycenaeans. The Ionians had also absorbed technologies for leather-making, spinning, weaving, and other crafts. They inherited as well knowledge of geography and navigation and the natural laws that apply to agriculture. Many of these ideas were passed on in the epic poems created by Homer and Hesiod during the mid-800s B.C.

Hesiod's poem *Works and Days*, for example, includes sections that are like a present-day farmer's almanac. There are simple instructions on what time of year to plow and plant the land and when to first "sharpen your sickle," as Hesiod put it, in preparation for harvesting grains.

In the famous poems the *Iliad* and the *Odyssey*, Homer presents some natural laws of navigation when he tells how early Greek sailors found their way to the Atlantic ocean. This information helped establish formal theories about a disk-shaped earth encircled by water.

Through poetry that was memorized and passed on from one generation to the next, Ionian (or Greek) colonists were no doubt stimulated to develop new ways of thinking. Citizens of Miletus, especially, lived in "a meeting place of ideas," as one historian described that rich, bustling trade center. Miletus and other port cities were terminals not only for Greek ships but also for Egyptian and Phoenecian ships. Caravan roads connected Ionian port cities with the land of Canaan, where Hebrew prophets lived and wrote books of the Bible. Both sea and land routes provided far-reaching communication with Persia, India, and China.

14

Many different customs, beliefs, and theories were brought to the Greeks of Ionia. With this intermingling of cultures, the Greeks were not bound by traditions and old ways of thinking. They felt free to seek new answers to ancient questions about the natural workings of the world. The pursuit of truth and reason became a noble venture.

THALES' ACHIEVEMENTS

Thales was born into this environment around 624 B.C. During his youth he developed a keen curiosity about mathematics and astronomy. He traveled to Egypt and the Near East to learn about geometry and to study the stars. According to legend, Thales became so absorbed in stargazing that he once fell into a ditch while walking along and staring up at the sky.

Through the centuries, Thales has been given credit for a number of accomplishments. He has been called the founder of magnetism. Apparently he discovered the magnetic properties of lodestone, an ore that attracts iron. He is also credited with being able to predict a total eclipse of the sun. But most science historians today do not believe such a feat would have been possible. The facts and theories needed to make such predictions were not discovered until years after Thales' time.

Nevertheless, Thales is also known as the first Greek astronomer and mathematician. He did bring from Egypt factual information about periodic eclipses of the sun. He also brought some practical knowledge of geometry. For example, he used Egyptian geometric rules to determine the distance of ships offshore and to measure the height of buildings. After solving such problems, it is said that Thales began to explain how he reached his solutions. Whether he actually developed theories behind geometric problems is uncertain, but the use of geometric facts led to the development of geometry as a science. Formal principles of geometry were spelled out by Pythagoras (pih THAG oh rus), the famous Greek mathematician of the next century, and later by Euclid in thirteen books on geometry that were continually in use until this century.

One major achievement that historians agree on is that Thales developed a theory about the origin of the earth. In his view, the earth was flat and floated on an ocean. Water, he believed, was the original substance from which all things materialized. He theorized that the earth, air, and all living things had begun as water and would, over time, change and become water once again.

Thales probably based his conclusions on easily observed facts. Water appears in three different forms—gas/vapor, liquid, and solid—and those forms change under various conditions, such as when ice and snow from the mountains melt in warmer weather or places. Thales no doubt also observed that water is necessary for life.

Significantly, Thales did not say that the gods were creators of life. He asked questions about the nature of the world and looked for facts to support his theory that the universe had been formed by a natural process. Thales set the stage for observing, recording, and categorizing factual information about the physical world. As the philosopher and mathematician Bertrand Russell once wrote, "Philosophers from Thales onwards have tried to understand the world." Thales has been given credit for taking the vital first steps in the development of science.

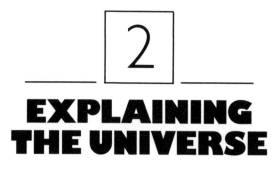

EXPLAINING THE UNIVERSE

As the Ionian philosophers tried to understand the world and its place in the universe, they studied changes in nature—in physical things. Thales and the philosophers who followed him posed such questions as: What is the origin of the universe? What is the world made of? Is there order in nature?

In their quest for answers the philosophers began to separate factual information from opinions or beliefs about creation. In effect, they used processes that are part of the scientific method of research, although the word *science* only developed much later. The scientific method today generally involves gathering facts, developing a theory, performing experiments to see if the theory is true, and then drawing conclusions. Although Greek philosophers collected factual information and developed many theories, they did not test their theories through experimentation. They did, however, try to explain their theories about things that they could not or had not seen.

Historians often refer to these ancient Greek philosophers as philosopher-scientists, since there was no clear distinction between the two fields of study. Many of these early scientists organized and wrote down their ideas about what the universe was made of and how it began. They were the first to put together a literature of science, which survived even after Greece itself declined. The writings contributed centuries later to the growth of science in the rest of Europe.

IDEAS ABOUT CREATION

One of the first to put his observations in writing was Anaximander. An astronomer and perhaps a pupil of Thales in Miletus, Anaximander believed that an unlimited number of worlds had been formed through a series of explosions. In his view our earth was created when materials spun off from the universe; the earth remained suspended within the universe, rotating freely and forever. The rotating motion, he thought, had caused the heaviest materials, such as rock, to fall to the center of the earth, which was shaped like a cylinder. Lighter materials, such as water and vapor, rose to the outer edges of the earth, and the sun, moon, and stars moved in circles around the cylinder.

Anaximander appears to have accepted Thales' idea that living organisms first came from water. But Anaximander also believed that the first organisms—sea animals—developed in husks or shells. Over time, the sun evaporated some of the water that covered the earth, and land appeared. The sea animals found their way to land, shed their husks, and adapted to new ways of life.

Anaximander, who believed that the universe was formed through a series of explosions and that life originated in the oceans

Anaximander theorized that humankind evolved from these sea animals. His ideas provided a basis for much later theories about evolution.

Another Ionian, Anaximenes (an ak SIM uh neez), who may have studied with Anaximander in Miletus, disagreed with the idea that life began in water. Rather, he theorized that all things had been created from air. How did he come to this conclusion? By observing condensation (thickening or compressing) and rarefaction (thinning) of air. Anaximenes believed that condensation produced first wind and clouds, then water, earth, and stone. Rarefaction, in his view, brought about fire.

To "prove" his theory about rarefaction, Anaximenes used a demonstration. He showed that when you purse your lips and blow compressed air, the air is cool; but when you open your mouth and exhale, dispersing or thinning the air, the air is warm. Thus rarefied, heated air could produce fire, Anaximenes said. In his view, air was the very soul of the earth, and all the universe breathed.

A later Ionian, Heraclitus (hehr ah KLY tus), who was born about 530 B.C., said that neither air or water was the basic element from which all things were created. Rather, he believed, all things on earth came from fire. He based this idea on the fact that fire consumes and changes things—it both destroys and creates something else as it burns. Fire, for example, could become gas, which then could condense to water. This led to his theory that everything in the universe was in a state of flux, or change. As Heraclitus explained it, "You can never step twice into the same river." In other words, a river is forever changing, so the second time you step into it, it is not the same.

Apparently Heraclitus spent most of his life developing his theories, including the theory that tension is a balancing force in nature. He believed that tension created a balance between opposites such as night and day, life and death, hot and cold. Many called Heraclitus' ideas "obscure," or hard to understand. In fact,

Heraclitus himself became known as "The Obscure." But many of his ideas about nature and the universe influenced later philosophers, especially Plato, whose philosophy included a theory to explain what things are—and are not.

MORE THEORIES

Theories about the universe were not developed only by the Ionians. Early scientists living in Greek colonies along the coasts of Italy and on the mainland of Greece were also making observations that led to ideas about creation. One of the most famous was Pythagoras, who settled in the Greek colony of Croton in southern Italy in the mid-500s B.C. Pythagoras is known for his school of mathematics, as described in Chapter 3. But his followers also put forth the idea that the earth is a planet. They theorized that the earth, along with other planets, orbits a fire in the center of the universe.

The Pythagorean theory said that the central fire is hidden from view on earth. Another planet called a counter-earth comes between the fire and the earth. Light from the fire reaches the earth by reflecting from the sun. Both the counter-earth and the earth move at the same speed as they orbit the central fire. When people can no longer see the reflected light of the fire, it is because their part of the earth has rotated away from the sun. The most important aspect of this theory was that it said that the earth rotates as it orbits, which led to later inquiries about the movements of planets.

In the century or so after Pythagoras' lifetime, many more Greek scientists wrote down their views on the nature of the universe. Xenophanes (zehn AH fun eez), for example, is said to have spent most of his life traveling, but he settled for a time in western Italy in the Greek colony of Elea. There he wrote about his views on the mixture of land and sea.

Like some of the other early scientists, Xenophanes believed that all things originated from water—or mud, as he put it. The earth, he said, had pulled away from the sea; as proof he pointed out the results of his careful investigations. He had found shells in mountain regions, prints of fish and other sea animals in rocks, and parts of marine life buried on land. His discoveries were a beginning of paleontology, the study of prehistoric life through fossils.

Another Greek colonist, Empedocles, who lived on the southern coast of Sicily, seems to have brought together many of the earlier theories about the makeup of the universe. Unlike the philosophers before him, he did not pick one element—water, air, fire, or earth/land—as a basic substance from which all things are made. Instead, Empedocles said that all things are composed of a combination of the four elements—earth, fire, air, and water.

In Empedocles' view, the four elements began in perfect balance. But the moving forces of love and strife (harmony and discord) ruled over the elements and brought about changes. Empedocles thought that any change in an object was due to the motion, or change in position, of the basic elements. His ideas were the first attempt to explain the principles of motion.

EARLY ATOMIC THEORIES

Near the end of the fifth century B.C., ideas about the basic properties of matter came closer to present-day views about the structure of matter. Democritus (dee MAHK rih tuhs), who lived from about 460 to 370 B.C. in the northern Aegean seaport of Abdera, rejected the idea that harmony and discord have an effect on mate-

Democritus believed that matter was composed of atoms.

rials. Instead, he used terms that are familiar today; he said that all things are made up of tiny particles called atoms.

Apparently Democritus adapted or enlarged upon ideas first put forth by his teacher, Leucippus, who left no written works. Democritus carried on Leucippus' atomic theory, explaining that atoms can not be changed. However, since atoms are of different sizes and shapes, they can combine to form objects with various properties. Democritus wrote that atoms combine in a similar way to form an infinite number of worlds in the universe, while the universe itself is made up of atoms floating in a vacuum, or void.

The possibility that there might be a vacuum, or nothingness, disturbed most other philosophers of the time. It was commonly accepted that the universe was fully occupied by matter. However, in the next century, Epicurus revived the theory that nothing exists except atoms and the void. Unlike Democritus, who believed that the shapes and forms of atoms are predetermined, Epicurus stated that atoms had come together by chance to create the various objects in the world.

In the first century B.C. the Roman poet Lucretius (lyew KREE shus) wrote a long poem "on the nature of things," in which he set forth the arguments of both Democritus and Epicurus. The poem's underlying theme is that the universe was created by the combining of atoms and not by the will or intervention of gods. Democritus' theory (borrowed or adapted from Leucippus) was preserved. Nearly two thousand years later, his ideas on the atom may have influenced the scientists of the 1800s who developed theories that eventually led to the atomic science of this century.

MATHEMATICIANS — GEOMETERS

Along with theories about the origins of the world, many Greek scientists also developed mathematical theories. For the early Greeks, mathematics was primarily geometry, which literally means "measuring the earth." The Greeks learned from the Egyptians how to use geometry to measure land areas for planting crops and laying out cities. Geometry was also used to measure such structures as palaces and temples. But the philosopher-scientists went a step further. They wanted to find out why the rules for measuring areas and shapes held true.

THE PYTHAGOREANS

A name closely linked with geometry is Pythagoras, who lived from about 560 to 500 B.C. Although born on the island of Samos, across the gulf from Miletus, Pythagoras is said to have traveled to Egypt, to Babylonia, and perhaps to India and Syria to study astronomy and geometry. He eventually settled in the Greek colony of Croton in southern Italy. There he set up a school that was an outgrowth of a religious order, or brotherhood, made up of his followers. Members of the Pythagorean Order were expected to refrain from eating meat, avoid alcohol, wear simple clothing, and go barefoot. The order welcomed women as well as men, but the group separated itself from the rest of society.

Students at the Pythagorean school had to live by strict rules since they were expected to develop pure bodies and minds. The mind, it was believed, could be purified through scientific study. Geometry and arithmetic (mathematics), music, and astronomy made up the curriculum. Mathematics was the most important field of study; Pythagoreans were probably the first to use the term *mathematike* to mean mathematics. Before the Pythagorean school, *mathema* had meant any type of learning.

In the study of mathematics, Pythagoreans emphasized clear thinking through **deductive reasoning**—reaching a conclusion by going from a general law to a specific or particular case. The school was an ideal setting to enlarge upon Pythagoras' theory that "all things are numbers." Pythagoreans appear to have reached this conclusion after observing mathematical relationships in music, in triangles, and in the patterns of orbiting stars and planets.

In music, Pythagoreans observed that the notes on the scale correspond to the lengths of vibrating strings or vibrating columns of air. For example, plucking on a stringed instrument will produce one note; if that string is reduced to half its length, the note will be an octave, or eight tones, higher. Pythagoras linked these intervals in music with number ratios. He realized that notes produce harmonious sounds. Thus, Pythagoras developed an idea about the

One of the many great discoveries of Pythagoras was the mathematical relationships among the tones of a musical scale.

numbers 12, 8, and 6. Because of their relationship to musical intervals, the numbers were said to be in "harmonic progression." Pythagoras extended this concept to geometrical forms. In fact, he claimed that the cube was in "geometric harmony" because of its twelve sides, eight angles, and six faces.

THE PYTHAGOREAN THEOREM
AND OTHER FINDINGS

The Pythagoreans were aware of the rule of right triangles that had been brought from Egypt. According to this rule, which was used to make corners square in buildings, one type of right triangle has sides three units, four units, and five units long. The angle between the two shorter sides is a right angle.

The Pythagoreans thought of each side of a right triangle as a side of a square. The area of a square can be found by multiplying a side by itself. The Pythagoreans developed the right angle rule, which says that in any right triangle, the area of the square on the longest side is equal to the sum of the areas of the squares on the other two sides. Later, this proof became known as the Pythagorean Theorem. (In geometry, a theorem is a statement that has to be proved.)

From the Pythagorean Theorem, followers of Pythagoras discovered that not all quantities can be stated as whole numbers. They found in working the equation for the right angle rule that the results include fractions. The study of fractions led later to the measurement of the five *regular solids*, so named because in each regular solid all the faces are equal in area and in shape. These solids are formed from triangles, squares, or pentagons (five-sided figures).

The Pythagoreans also studied curved lines and developed mathematical theories about the basic order of the **cosmos**. They were the first to use the term *cosmos* to mean an orderly universe

The five regular solids.
Do you know their names?

—the idea that the world is a harmonious system—that could be expressed in numbers. The Pythagoreans also gave mystical values to certain numbers and shapes and their occurrence in the universe. Some numbers are almost holy or magical, they said.

Historians say that the Pythagoreans were probably the first to split science from philosophy, establishing two different kinds of thought. One was based on materialism, or trying to understand the physical properties of objects in terms of numbers and measurements. The other was the concept of deductive reasoning not only to solve mathematical problems but also to "prove" a variety of beliefs and idealistic notions. Plato, the famous philosopher who lived from 427 to about 347 B.C., used deductive reasoning in arguments to prove his theory of ideas. He believed that it was misleading to observe and investigate nature and to perform experiments. True reality, he said, could be found only in learning and understanding ideas.

Pythagorean ideas about mathematical relationships influence scientific thinking to this day. The Pythagorean school spread the idea that specific laws determine how matter will develop and form and that those laws can be described in mathematical relationships.

OTHER MATHEMATICIANS

Hippocrates (hih PAHK ruh teez) of Chios in the mid-400s B.C. used Pythagorean concepts in his work. Hippocrates moved from Chios to Athens, the center of education and philosophy during the so-called Age of Pericles. The ruler Pericles encouraged people to pursue the arts and sciences.

Hippocrates founded a mathematics school that was renowned for two hundred years. He put together the first known book on geometry, creating an order for the many geometric theorems developed in the previous century.

Hippocrates also studied the geometrical problems that faced mathematicians of that time. One of those problems was squaring the circle, or finding a square equal in area to the area of a circle. Although he was unable to solve the problem, he did discover the area of a lune, a shape that looks like the first or last quarter of the moon.

No one knows for certain how Hippocrates found the area of a lune, a most difficult geometric problem. But his work influenced Hippias of Elis, a mathematician and teacher who lived in the area of mainland Greece known as the Peloponnesus. Hippias began a new branch of geometry in which the measurements of higher curves are found with mathematical equations and without the use of ruler and compass.

At about the same time, Democritus of Abdera, who had developed the early atomic theory of the universe, wrote four texts on geometry. He explained how to find the areas of cones and pyramids.

Another great name of this period was Eudoxus of Cnidus. He made basic contributions to geometry with his definition of proportion and method of exhaustion. These became tools for calculating the area of a circle and the volume of a sphere, pyramid, and cone.

ADVANCES IN GEOMETRY

Mathematics—that is, geometry—continued to advance in the latter part of the third century through the first century B.C., often called the Alexandrian period. This period was named for Alexander the Great, whose armies established a Greek empire that reached into Macedonia, deep into western Asia, and into Egypt. The Egyptian capital city, Alexandria, was named for him. He spread Greek culture and language throughout the vast territory taken over by his armies. The period following Alexander's became known as the Hellenistic Age, meaning that people of other cultures and races adopted Greek ways.

Dozens of mathematicians studied and worked at Alexandria during the Hellenistic period. Among them was Apollonius, who was born about 220 B.C. He is remembered for his geometry text *On Conics*, which explained the curves that result when a cone is sectioned off (cut through) by a plane or straight line. Apollonius gave names to the various curves—ellipse, parabola, and hyperbo-

la—that are still used today in higher mathematics. Understanding the curves, especially the ellipse, helped European mathematicians of the late 1600s construct theories about the orbits of planets.

Euclid, one of the greatest scientists of the Hellenistic period, founded a mathematical school at Alexandria, where the famous Museum, or research library, had been established. Little is certain about Euclid's life. He was probably educated in mathematics at the Academy in Athens and then later moved to Alexandria. He became known as Euclid of Alexandria. There he wrote the thirteen books of the *Elements*—a geometry text—and taught a few dedicated students.

One story about him goes that a Greek king asked him whether there was a shorter way to learn geometry than by working step by step through the *Elements*. Euclid supposedly told the king that there was no royal road to geometry. In other words, all people—even royalty—had to master mathematics by the same difficult route.

With the *Elements*, Euclid created a system for the study of geometry that led some historians to call him the "father of geometry." For two thousand years his texts formed the basis for geometry. To this day Euclid's work influences the way problems are solved and how logic is used.

Euclid, the
father of geometry

4

STAR GAZERS

Many of the ancient Greek philosophers, such as Thales, Anaximander, and Anaximenes, applied their knowledge of mathematics to the field of astronomy. In their observations and studies, they used a simple instrument called a **gnomon.** Long used by the Egyptians, the gnomon was a measured stick planted upright in an open, smooth area of ground so that it could cast a shadow from sunrise to sunset. (The pointer or triangular piece on a sundial is a gnomon.)

By observing shadows cast by a gnomon, astronomers could calculate the lengths of the days and the year. They knew when "real" noon would occur each day—the varying time when the sun is highest in the sky and when the gnomon casts a minimal shadow. The gnomon also helped astronomers determine the solstices, the longest and shortest days of the year.

Such findings probably led ancient scientists to some understanding of the angled path that the sun seems to travel in the sky each year. They also were able to identify the times of year now called the equinoxes, when the sun's center is directly over the equator. Since the center of the sun crosses the equator twice a year, there are two equinoxes, one in spring and the other in fall; at those times, days and nights are almost equal in length.

PLANETARY THEORIES

As the study of astronomy advanced, a variety of theories about the universe, planets, and stars were put forth. For example, Anaxagoras, who studied in Athens around 480 B.C., said that when the universe was created it was separated into two layers and went into rotation. As the whirling motion slowed, stones tore loose from the outer layer and fell to the earth as meteors, an idea that laid a foundation for later studies in meteorology.

Anaxagoras went further, stating that the moon had "on its surface plains, mountains, and ravines." He theorized correctly that the moon received its light from the sun and was the closest heavenly body to the earth. The eclipse of the moon came about because of the "interposition [coming between] of the earth," he rightly noted, and the eclipse of the sun was due to the "interposition of the moon."

Eudoxus of Cnidus—the geometer—was also an astronomer. He was especially interested in the movements of celestial bodies. He wrote several books on the subject and concluded that the sun, the moon, and each of the planets move in a series of spheres or circles at several different speeds, each around its own axis. His scheme was complex, but it was based on a sound mathematical explanation for the movements of celestial bodies. To this day, astronomical instruments are based on Eudoxus' models of spheres. He also laid a foundation for later scientific studies in weather prediction.

ADVANCED IDEAS

Astronomy continued to advance with the work of other scientists such as Aristarchus of Samos. Aristarchus probably lived around 310 to 230 B.C. and studied at Alexandria. He made the first scientific attempt to measure the sizes of the sun and moon and their distances from earth. He was able to calculate the distance of the moon from earth but was incorrect in his conclusion that the sun is eighteen times farther from earth than the moon. In reality, the sun is almost 400 times farther away. Still, his methods for measuring helped later scientists in their calculations of the distances and sizes of celestial bodies.

One of Aristarchus' most important contributions to astronomy was his theory that the earth revolves around a stationary sun. His view was not accepted, since most philosophers of his time believed that the center of the universe was an immobile earth. An additional problem was the fact that no one could observe any change in the positions of stars, which would be likely if the earth orbited the sun, it was thought. As a result, Aristarchus' ideas were put aside and almost forgotten.

Seventeen centuries later, in A.D. 1543, the Polish astronomer Nicholas Copernicus expanded on Aristarchus's theory. Copernicus said that the earth rotated on its axis and along with other planets revolved around the sun. Because the ideas of the early Greek astronomer were so much like those of Copernicus, some historians refer to Aristarchus as "the Copernicus of Antiquity."

GREAT ASTRONOMERS

Hipparchus of Nicaea, who was born about 190 B.C., has been called "the greatest astronomer of antiquity," "a lover of truth," and "a scientist of the highest type." Why all the praise? Because so much of his work affected astronomy for centuries.

As a young man Hipparchus moved to Rhodes, where he built an observatory. There he named and catalogued about 850 stars. Although others had compiled similar catalogues, he was the first to note the positions of stars by lines of latitude and longitude. He improved the instruments used in astronomy at that time and developed a mathematical table to compute the stars' positions.

*Hipparchus,
the greatest astronomer
of the ancient world*

One tedious job undertaken by Hipparchus was to compile the records of astronomers before him. He noted changes that had taken place in the positions of stars over a period of about 150 years. While making comparisons, he discovered a process now called the precession of the equinoxes. During this process some stars seem to change position in relation to certain fixed points in the sky. These changes, Hipparchus realized, came about because of the way the earth rotates on its axis—the imaginary line that connects the north and south poles. The earth also tilts slightly in relation to an imaginary line that joins the earth's center with the center of the sun. As the earth makes its elliptical orbit around the sun and rotates like a top on its axis, the stars seem to move, even though in reality they remain in one place. But the tilt of the earth in relation to the stars does change very slightly over a cycle of 26,000 years. As a result, the equinoxes (spring and fall) occur a little earlier each year.

Hipparchus was also able to make more accurate measurements of the distances of the sun and moon from earth than had been possible before. In addition, his theory of the movement of the planets helped astronomers in his time and after to predict within an hour the eclipses of the moon.

Most of what is known about Hipparchus comes from Claudius Ptolemy (TAHL eh mih), a great astronomer who lived from about A.D. 100 to 170. Ptolemy based many of his ideas on the research of Hipparchus. In his writings, Ptolemy referred often to the earlier astronomer's theories.

Some of Ptolemy's writings include descriptions of his experiments with optics and how light rays refract—seem to bend—when passing from one medium to another. In a book entitled *Optics*, Ptolemy explained how starlight is refracted by the atmosphere, making a star appear to be higher in the sky than it really is.

Ptolemy's greatest achievement by far was a thirteen-volume

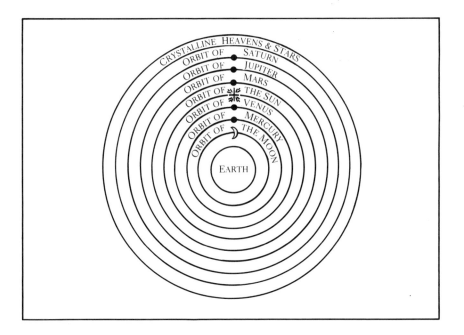

The universe according to Ptolemy

text that was first called *A Mathematical Composition*. The work later became known as the *Almagest*, a title that combines Arabic and Latin words and roughly means "a great compilation."

In the *Almagest*, Ptolemy brought together the most important findings of Greek astronomers from the fifth century B.C. to his own day. He preserved and elaborated on earlier ideas and expanded Hipparchus' catalogue of stars from 850 to well over 1,000. His work also included a description of a mathematical arrangement of the stars.

A number of instruments that ancient astronomers used were described in the *Almagest*. One device was made with outer and

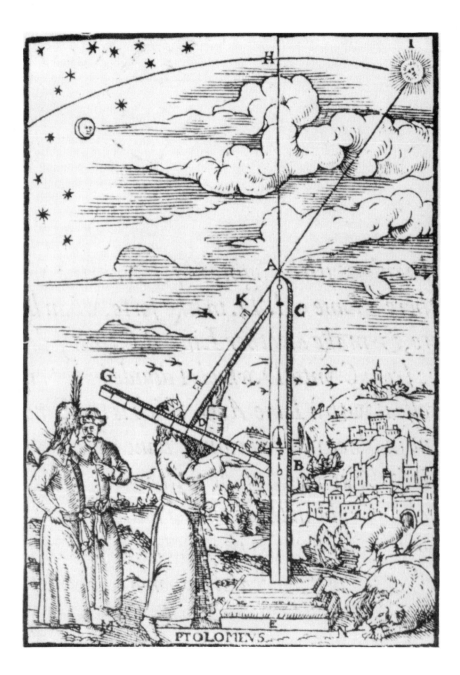

PTOLOMEVS.

inner metal rings; the inner one was marked with degrees for measuring the distance of stars and planets. Another instrument was a block of wood with an eyehole—the block slid back and forth in a wooden frame and was used to determine the width of the sun's disk.

The main focus of Ptolemy's writing was on his theory explaining how celestial bodies orbit the earth. Ptolemy, like other scientists of his time, rejected the notion of a rotating earth, saying instead that the earth was stationary and was the center of the universe. The moon, sun, and stars, Ptolemy said, circled the earth. According to a theory that Ptolemy developed, the planets also circled the earth at various speeds, each in its own sphere. Ptolemy's system of planetary movements was so well accepted that it remained unchanged until the seventeenth century.

Ptolemy using an instrument
to study the heavens

5

GEOGRAPHERS

As early Greek scientists studied the stars and the planets, many also were concerned about the earth's surface. The study of land surfaces—finding the heights of mountains, depths of valleys, volumes of lakes, and similar measurements—became known as *geography*. The term is, of course, closely akin to geometry, the rules for measuring areas.

Some of the earliest geographical information was presented in Homer's epic poem the *Odyssey*, which tells of the ten-year wanderings of Odysseus. The poem contains descriptions of land formations—mountains, valleys, rivers, and bays—and such Aegean cities as Mycenae, Athens, and Thebes. Various kinds of goods shipped over land and sea routes are also described.

Over the centuries, explorers have tried to trace the travels of Odysseus and in some cases have found places and routes described in the epic poem. During the 1960s, for example, one adventurer spent several months following what he believed was the route Homer had created in the *Odyssey*. Whether such a route actually exists is still a matter of debate, however, since many of the place names in the poem were taken from folklore.

THE FIRST MAPS

Geography involves map-making. Information for early maps often depended on daily logs of sailors. Geographers also created maps based on their own travels and on reports from merchants and wandering storytellers who came to Greek ports.

The first world map was supposedly created by the astronomer Anaximander of Miletus. In the center of his map was Greek territory. The rest of Europe and Asia surrounded Greece, and the entire land area was encircled by an ocean.

This concept may have been the basis for a more advanced map by Hecataeus (hek ah TEE us) of Miletus, who lived during the sixth century B.C. At that time, ships from Miletus were sailing the Mediterranean and Black seas; travelers were bringing back a great variety of information about distant peoples and lands. Hecataeus evidently used such knowledge as well as information gathered from his own broad travels to create a map showing a flat earth and land areas labeled "Europe," "Asia," and "Africa." Following common practice, Hecataeus' earth was disk-shaped and surrounded by a body of water called Oceanus.

APPLYING GEOGRAPHIC RESEARCH

Hecataeus also compiled information to write the first geography "book," only parts of which remain. During antiquity, a book was actually a roll of thin paper. The paper was made from **papyrus**, a grasslike plant that grows in marshes. Papyrus leaves were split into very thin strips, then moistened with muddy water that acted like glue and held the strips together in sheets. The sheets were pressed and dried in the sun. After authors wrote their texts on papyrus, about twenty sheets were glued together and rolled on a cylinder to form a "book." Long texts often required several such rolls. Since the papyrus sheets were brittle and easily damaged, very few ancient writings have been preserved.

Along with his geographic research, Hecataeus studied how the physical environment—the geography of an area—affected people of various regions. Hecataeus' ideas were a basis for further research by the famous Greek historian Herodotus (he ROD oh tus) of the fifth century B.C. Herodotus theorized that nature and custom determine how people live and that geographical changes can alter people's customs.

The ancient Greeks applied geographic information in other ways as well. Trade, exploration, and military conquests, for example, often depended on sea route information and on descriptions of land areas, on what natural resources were available, and on what kind of crops were grown.

Knowing the locations and layouts of cities was a great help to Greek citizens who traveled for pleasure. One geographer prepared written guides to Greek cities. The guides described historic sites and monuments and were used by people who led visitors on tours of cities, much as guides direct tourists today.

A SCIENTIFIC APPROACH
TO GEOGRAPHY

With the development of astronomy in ancient Greece, a more scientific approach to geography became possible. In map-making, geographers located places on earth by finding the positions of celestial bodies on a sphere. Then they related these positions to the meridian (the imaginary line connecting the north and south poles) and to the lines of latitude. The Greeks were the first to develop maps with lines of latitude and longitude.

Eratosthenes (air uh TAHS thuh nees) who lived from about 275 to 195 B.C., was one of the most scientific geographers of

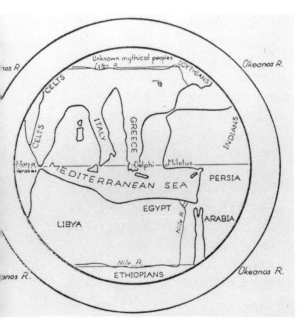

Left: *The first known world map, created by Anaximander. The original was obviously in Greek. Below: The world according to Eratosthenes. The names were originally in Greek.*

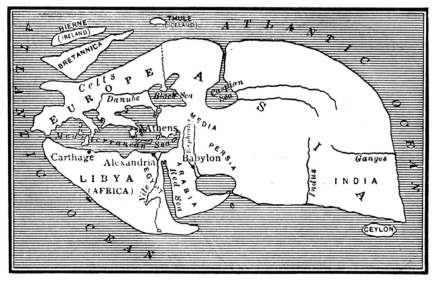

ancient Greece. Like many other scientists in Alexandria, Eratosthenes studied at the Museum, where he eventually became the director. With his wide-ranging knowledge of literature, mathematics, and astronomy, Eratosthenes made numerous contributions to geography. He wrote a text that was the first to provide a mathematical basis for geography and to describe the world as a globe.

One of Eratosthenes' most important feats was his attempt to find the circumference of the world, which he determined to be about 29,000 miles (47,000 km) in today's units of measurement. His calculation came very close to that of modern geographers, who have measured the earth's circumference over the poles to be 24,819 miles (39,934 km). From the circumference, Eratosthenes calculated the diameter of the earth to be approximately 7,850 miles (12,600 km), very close to the correct polar diameter of about 7,900 miles (13,000 km).

Few of Eratosthenes' writings remain, but his work became the foundation for studies by later scholars such as Strabon, who was born about 64 B.C. Strabon came from a wealthy family and was well traveled and well educated; he studied in Rome and at the great library in Alexandria. He is remembered for his huge volume *Geography*, a work that Strabon himself described as *colossurgia*, or colossal. To prepare such a text today, a geographer would probably need many research assistants and the support of a major university.

Strabon recorded physical aspects of the earth, such as the location of mountains, rivers, and cities. He also provided a great

A section of one of Strabon's maps. The Nile runs up the middle.

Didymæ

Pharos

Canobos
Heracleoticũ
Bolbitinum oftium
Sebẽnticum c.ftiam
Pineptimj oftium
folcos Pfeudoft
Pathmiticõ oftium
Mendefiũ oft.
Taniticũ oft.
Pelufiacũ oft.
Pelfium

Bryxicæ

Antaeopolis

Iudęæ pars

Derris

Cherfonefus parua
Plinthine
Chimo
Glauciũ, τομου

Maria
lacus

Alexãdria

Memphis

Tanis

Gerrã

Sirbonis palus

Mareotus

goniatæ

ARABIAE

Bubaftus

Bufiris

Petreæ
pars

ofoditæ
Maftitæ

Mœridis
lacus

Sathiã regio

Arfinoe

Babylon

Troicus

Arfinoe

Sinus Ara
bicus
Saffirena

Nitriotæ

Clyfma

Alabaftrenus

AEGYPTVS

Niluf fl.

Drepanum
promont.

mons

AR

Oafitæ

Libya montes

Porphurieus

Miformus

Philoteras

Aias mons
Acabe mons

RI

Ptolemais

Thebais

Coptos

Thebæ

Nechefia

Libyægyptij

deal of information about such phenomena as earthquakes, volcanos, and erosion. He included as well descriptions of such industries as salt mining and glassmaking. Strabon's special interest, however, was in the people of particular regions—how they lived, what they wore and ate, and other characteristics. His book is full of descriptions of various groups of people and their customs.

A little over one hundred years later, another major book, also called *Geography*, was written by the astronomer Ptolemy, who worked for the most part in Alexandria. He is remembered for bringing astronomy and geography together in a scientific way. His book on geography listed cities and other places in the known world along with their latitudes and longitudes. Maps and charts showed how to represent a curved earth on a flat plane. The text contained a number of location errors, but it was the first major outline of the world as understood in antiquity.

6

PHYSICIANS
AND ANATOMISTS

Greeks of the sixth century B.C. knew very little about the causes of disease. No one had yet discovered that some bacteria and germs can infect the body. There was also only slight knowledge of anatomy and physiology—the makeup of the body and how it works.

Early Greek medical scientists did not study body organs since they had a distaste for dissecting—cutting open—human corpses. It was thought to be an offense against the gods. Not until the Hellenistic period, when doctors trained with Egyptians, who had long used dissection in medical research, did Greek scientists begin to accept dissection as a way to learn about diseases and other physical ailments.

Still, there was some general knowledge of the human body's bone and muscle structure, particularly from athletics, an important part of ancient Greek life. Based on careful observation and experience, trainers at *gymnasia*—exercise—knew how to treat sprains, bone fractures, and dislocations.

The ancient Greeks also had an understanding of how to treat wounds suffered by soldiers at war. Some of the earliest descriptions of battlefield surgery and the use of anesthetics appear in

Homer's *Iliad*, which tells about a war centuries earlier between the Greeks and the people of Troy on the coast of Asia Minor.

When it came to diseases of the body, treatments were more closely tied to religion and philosophy than to direct knowledge of how the body functioned. Temple priests were often consulted for "cures" since it was generally believed that disease was due to the anger of the gods. The priests would cast "spells" as remedies for illnesses, or they would require sick patients to make offerings to the gods. Diseases were also treated with diet and exercise. And early physicians sometimes prescribed herbs and bloodletting to combat sickness.

MEDICAL SCHOOLS

During the fifth century B.C., some progress was made in Greek medical science. By that time, due to the guidance of one of its chief rulers, Pericles, Athens had become a center of learning. Four schools of medicine had been established. One of the most influential was on the island of Cos off the southeastern coast of Asia Minor. This school was founded by Hippocrates, whose name is still closely associated with medical practice today.

Another school in Asia Minor was at Cnidus; two others were in Greek colonies at Croton in Italy and in Sicily. Usually, medical knowledge was combined with philosophical theories. For example, the physicians who trained at Croton followed Pythagorean theories about the balance of forces within a body. An imbalance in those forces was believed to cause most physical ailments.

Hippocrates and those who studied at his school at Cos were responsible for freeing medicine from most philosophical theories and religious beliefs. Making careful observations and recording factual information—essential activities for any science—were part of the Hippocratic teachings. In a collection of writings called the *Hippocratic Corpus*, which was written by Hippocrates and his

Doctors today still pledge to uphold
standards of medical conduct developed
by Hippocrates nearly 2,500 years ago.

later followers, there are many references to the rational understanding of the human body and disease.

One essay in the *Hippocratic Corpus* argued against the idea
that some diseases were "sacred," that they were somehow caused
by the gods. The writer attacked the widely accepted notion that
epilepsy was brought about because a person was possessed by
demons. All diseases were actually the result of natural causes; the
origin of epilepsy, "like that of other diseases, lies in heredity," the
follower of Hippocrates wrote.

EARLY MEDICAL PRACTICE

One of the most important contributions of the Hippocratic school
was to set standards for doctors. The Hippocratic Oath has been a
guide for medical practitioners for more than two thousand years.
In essence, in taking the oath, a physician promises to be honest
with patients, to protect and preserve life, and to keep information
about patients private.

Honesty with patients was an essential part of prognosis—
forecasting the outcome of an illness, especially fatal diseases. This
meant that a doctor had to understand the symptoms of a specific
disease and how the disease might progress. "For in this way you
will justly win respect and be an able physician," Hippocrates
taught. An essay called "Prognostic," credited to Hippocrates,
advised physicians that "the longer time you plan to meet each
emergency, the greater your power to save those who have a
chance of recovery, while you will be blameless if you learn and
declare beforehand those who will die and those who will get better."

Even though little was known about anatomy, doctors had to
have a general theory about how the body worked in order to
practice medicine. They based their practices on a doctrine of
humors, or liquids—an old idea tied to philosophy. Although the

doctrine of humors has no place in modern medical science, it was accepted in medicine for more than twenty centuries. Perhaps this was because the Hippocratic school tried to explain the theory in a rational way.

According to the doctrine, the body contains four fluids: blood, phlegm, and yellow and black biles. Good health is possible if the four humors are in proper proportion to one another. Too much or too little of one of the liquids will lead to some type of illness. The humors are affected by climate and diet, the Hippocratic school taught. Doctors who moved to a new area to practice were advised to take note of what effects the local food and water, winds, dry or wet climate, and seasonal changes had on the people of a region.

Doctors who followed Hippocratic ideas were expected to observe and record the facts about a case and draw conclusions from the compiled information. Those conclusions could then be applied when treating similar cases. The remedies most often prescribed were rest and diet. Herbs were also used for medicinal purposes. Doctors often depended on nature to heal as well. A common expression was "Time is the great physician."

UNDERSTANDING ANATOMY
AND DISEASE

Although Hippocrates and his followers investigated anatomy, no systematic study of body structure took place until the third century B.C. During that period scientists at the Museum in Alexandria were free of the religious beliefs that banned dissection.

One scientist who studied and worked at the Museum was Herophilus, an anatomist—one who analyzes the anatomy of the human body. Herophilus discovered techniques for dissecting corpses, and he described and named many of the organs he found in the human body. For example, he pointed out that there is a

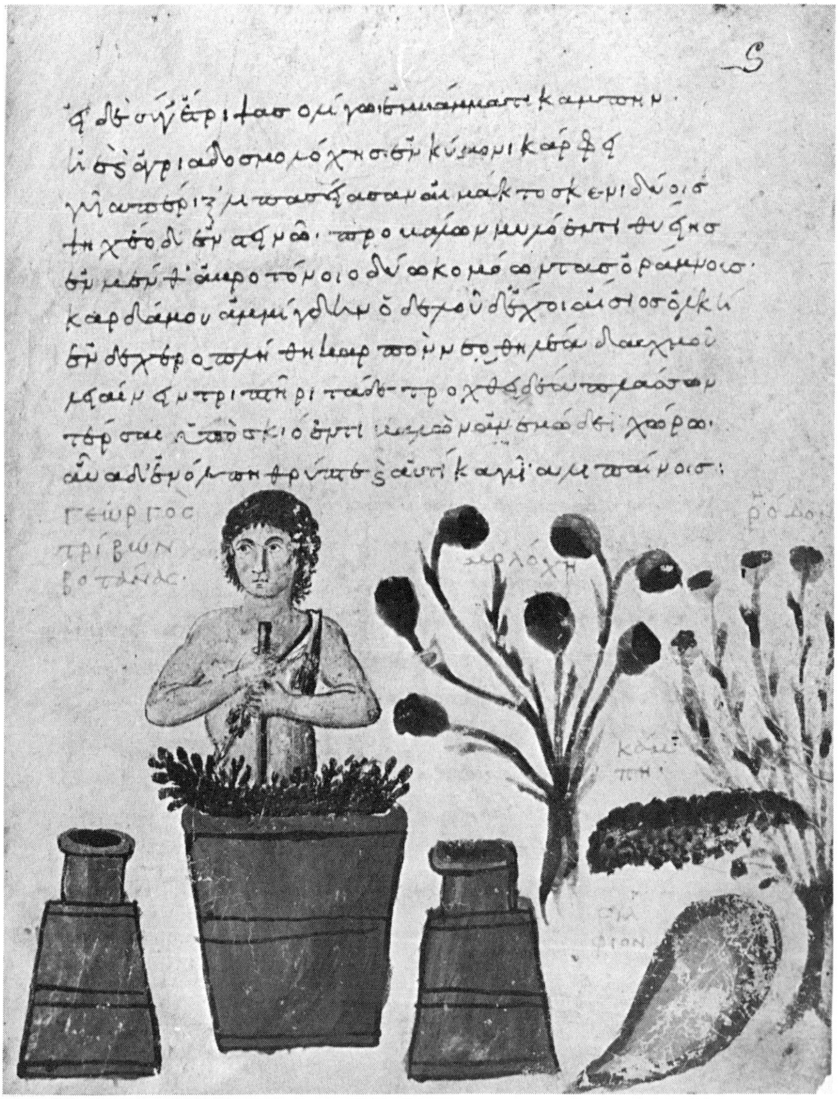

Herbs were often prescribed
for medicinal purposes.

clear difference between arteries and veins. He also made a distinction between tendons and nerves in the body, and he carefully described the makeup of the brain. Herophilus understood correctly that the brain is the center of the nervous system (not the heart, as was previously believed), and he showed how nerves connect with the brain through the spinal cord.

Another anatomist of the period was Erasistratus. He studied in Athens and continued the work of Herophilus. But Erasistratus was more interested in finding the causes of diseases. To do so, he conducted post-mortems—dissecting bodies of people who had just died. These autopsies helped him to recognize injuries or changes in organs of the body and thus to determine the possible causes of death.

During the two to three centuries after Hippocrates, many other scientists experimented with various aspects of medicine, including surgery. None of the physicians became well known, but they continued work in clinical cases, recording histories of illnesses and their outcomes. There were many studies of toxic plants to find antidotes and to prevent poisoning. Murder, execution, and accidental death by poisoning were common in ancient Greece, and many rulers feared that they would be assassinated with poison in their food or drink.

With the advances in the study of anatomy, early Greek physicians learned about the pulse and discovered how to measure it. This information could be used to diagnose illnesses. Medical practices were also influenced by a better understanding of how the structure and function of animal organs compared with those of human organs. At the same time botanists—those who study plant life—were putting together information about herbs that could be used for healing purposes or to reduce pain.

Not until the second century A.D. did Galen bring together the biological and medical information of ancient Greece. Galen was a Greek surgeon who lived in Rome most of his life, but he had

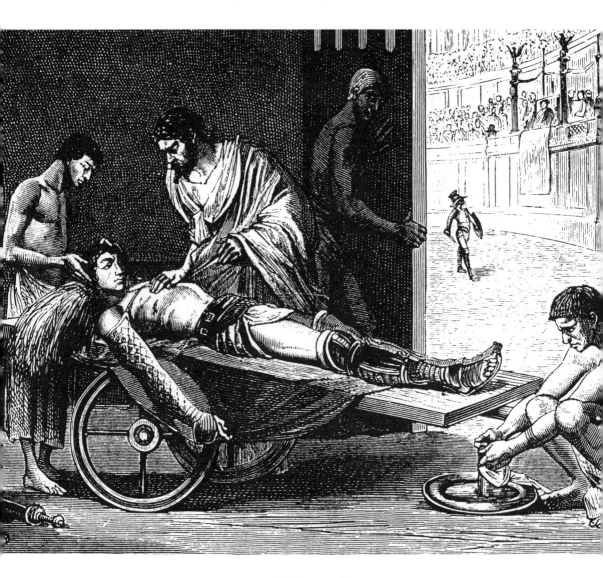

Galen tending to
a wounded gladiator

visited and studied at the Alexandria medical school. There he collected information about earlier achievements in anatomy, physiology, biology, and botany, and he applied that knowledge in his own experiments and theories. As a result, he developed a physiological system—a scheme for the way organs and other parts of the human body function. He is remembered in particular for showing that blood flows through the arteries rather than air, as had been thought up to that time.

Galen also wrote several hundred texts on medical science, which included not only his own findings but also those of earlier scientists. His books were popular and were translated into several languages. About eighty-five of his texts were preserved in spite of wars and other disasters. The ideas that Galen had compiled became a basis for medical theories developed by later physicians and anatomists.

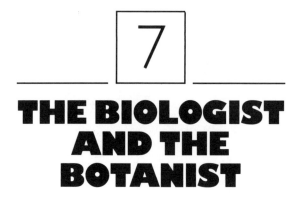

THE BIOLOGIST
AND THE
BOTANIST

Aristotle is a well-known name in ancient history. He has been called "the most scholarly and learned of the ancient Greek philosophers." One historian noted that "Aristotle was in many ways the most remarkable of Greek thinkers." Another writer called him "the most significant figure in Greek science."

Almost everyone who has written about Aristotle has described him in superlative terms. Often he is remembered for his philosophical ideas and methods of reasoning. But he also added greatly to scientific knowledge. Aristotle compiled information about every known field of study up to that time.

FROM STUDENT TO TEACHER

Born in 384 B.C. in a small Greek town near Macedonia, Aristotle moved to Athens when he was seventeen or eighteen years old to enroll at Plato's Academy, or school. He was Plato's brightest student and was connected with the Academy for about twenty years, leaving only after Plato died.

For a time Aristotle lived in Asia Minor, but he was asked to come to Macedonia to tutor the teenage Alexander, who later became the conqueror Alexander the Great. After Alexander took

Aristotle was arguably the most important thinker
who ever lived. He was a biologist, cosmologist, philosopher, social theorist, logician, and literary theorist.

over the rule from his father, who was assassinated, Aristotle went back to Athens. There he set up his own school of philosophy in a garden area named the Lyceum.

At the Lyceum, Aristotle often taught his students while walking with them in *peripatoi*, or covered areas of the garden. Because of this practice Aristotle and his followers became known as Peripatetics ("walkers-around"). The Peripatetic School attracted students ranging in age from those in their late teen years or early twenties to those as old as Aristotle himself.

During the time when he was at the Lyceum, Aristotle's teachings and writings reflected the influence of Plato. He accepted Plato's idea that the universe had a soul, and like Plato, he looked for perfection, or the "divine," in nature. Following Plato's example, Aristotle also rejected the theory that all things are made of atoms. Rather, he accepted the idea that all substances are made up of various combinations of the four elements—earth, air, water, and fire. In addition, he claimed that there is another element, called ether, that is the basic substance of stars and planets. Aristotle reasoned that since celestial bodies are perfect, they had to be made of an element quite different from the other four.

Aristotle taught that everything had its place in the world scheme. To understand that scheme, he believed it was necessary to know physics, which he defined as the nature and purpose of things. If birds fly, for example, it is because they are designed to fly—it is their nature. If some people are slaves, it is because it was determined beforehand; it is their purpose to serve, according to Aristotle.

Aristotle's teachings about the nature and purpose of the world were like a religion—a philosophical view—and were not based on the kind of observation and experiment that marked his research in other fields. But Aristotle used logical reasoning in his writings and teachings—a factor that helped keep his ideas alive for centuries.

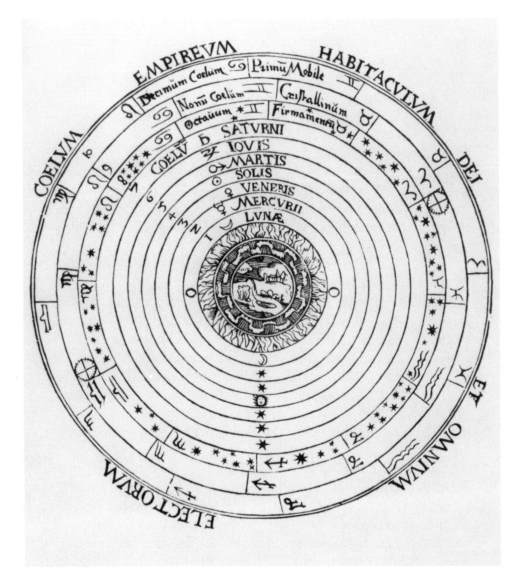

Aristotle's scheme of the universe.
The earth is at the center.

Aristotle's methods of reasoning included the use of **syllogisms.** In a syllogism, a conclusion can be drawn from two premises, or statements, that are assumed to be true. For example, the premises could be: 1) all animals die, and 2) a dog is an animal. Therefore, it can logically be concluded that a dog will die.

SCIENTIFIC RESEARCH

Even though he made use of the syllogism, Aristotle understood that one can hardly know the general without knowing the specifics. So he used another type of logic, too, called **inductive reasoning.** With inductive reasoning, general conclusions or principles develop from specific cases. Aristotle used such logic in his biological work.

First, though, he stressed the need to experiment and to make observations in nature. This was contrary to Plato's teaching that experiments show disrespect for the divine. It was also a departure from Aristotle's own ideas about the nature and purpose of the world. In biological research Aristotle pointed out the importance of making one's own discoveries, and he warned against accepting without question the research of others. He collected information, then analyzed and classified it. In short, he developed a research system that applied to all learning. Because of this accomplishment, he later became known as "the father of the scientific method."

Aristotle's contributions to biological science were tremendous. With the aid of his students, to whom he assigned research projects, Aristotle was the first to organize scientific information on animals and plants. Not only did he classify over five hundred animals, but he also described in several books many animal structures and how certain land and sea animals function and reproduce.

One of his most important investigations was the careful observation of developing chicks. He provided instructions for carrying out such an experiment: "Take twenty or more eggs and let them be incubated by two or more hens. Then each day, from the second to that of hatching, remove an egg, break it, and examine it." He described each stage of development, explaining that within a ten-day-old egg, "the chick and all its parts are distinctly visible." In his writings, Aristotle compared the chick with the human embryo, noting that it lies in the egg "in the same way the infant lies within its mother's womb." He also saw many similarities between human and animal anatomy. For example, he pointed out that nails were like animal claws and a hand like "a crab's nipper."

Aristotle's *History of Animals*—which some historians consider his most important biological work—is full of descriptions of animal and fish life. Some accounts were so carefully done that they compare favorably to modern studies of this type.

ARISTOTLE'S SUCCESSOR

Besides research on animal life, the study of plant life—botany—was also part of the curriculum at Aristotle's Lyceum. Theophrastus, one of Aristotle's students, was the expert on botany. He also gained expertise and wrote on such subjects as mineralogy, geography, astronomy, mathematics, and medicine.

Only twelve or thirteen years younger than his teacher, Theophrastus worked with Aristotle for more than twenty years. The two became good friends. But Theophrastus did not accept all of Aristotle's teachings. He often worked independently, and like any true scientist he questioned many of the master's ideas on the universe.

Theophrastus eventually was chosen to be director of the Lyceum when Aristotle was forced to leave Athens. The rulers of Athens believed that Aristotle did not show reverence for the gods. An earlier philosopher, Socrates, had received a death sentence for the same charge. In order to escape that fate, Aristotle fled to a distant city, where he died not long afterward.

As Theophrastus continued the work of the Lyceum, he also went on with his own research. He examined the smallest details of plants and recorded where they grew and how they might be used (for example, as pain-killers). He was particularly interested in how plants reproduce and what makes seeds grow, drawing his conclusions from evidence he found by observing nature.

In his book *The History of Plants*, Theophrastus explained that trees and plants originate "from seed, from a root, from a piece torn off, from a branch or twig, from the trunk itself; or again from small pieces into which the wood is cut up (for some trees can be produced even in this manner). Of these methods spontaneous growth comes first . . . but growth from seed or root would seem most natural; indeed these methods too may be called spontaneous; wherefore they are found even in wild kinds, while the remaining methods depend on human skill or at least on human choice."

As a botanist, Theophrastus needed technical terms to help him name various parts of plants or to describe plant development. But few botanical terms existed. So Theophrastus created special meanings for Greek words already in use. The Greek word *carpos*, for example, means "fruit"; from this word comes the term *carpel*, a botanical name for part of a flower. He also named many plants. Modern botanists still use some of those names.

Perhaps the most important botanical work of Theophrastus was his classification of plants. Like Aristotle before him, Theophrastus made careful and accurate observations. As he recorded and described each plant, he categorized it as an herb, an undershrub, a shrub, or a tree—the four main categories for plants that he created. The methods he used to distinguish among types of plants are still valid today.

THE "PURISTS" VS. THE PRACTICAL SCIENTISTS

From Thales to Theophrastus, ancient Greeks considered the study of "pure" science to be a noble pursuit, one to which they dedicated most of their energies over a lifetime. But many of these early philosophers thought it degrading to apply science—that is, to use knowledge about how nature works to make machines, household devices, and other practical items. Such activities, it was thought, were fit only for "base mortals" or slaves. People of high intellect were expected to use their minds, not their hands, in their life's work.

The great teacher Socrates of Athens, who lived during the fourth century B.C., was even against the study of natural phenomena—the workings of the physical world. He claimed that people would be better off seeking truth and learning how to deal honestly and peacefully with one another. Because Socrates was more concerned about moral values than about understanding how nature works, his teachings marked a great change in philosophy. From Socrates' time on, most philosophers concentrated their studies either on morality and achieving perfection or on the workings of nature, although a few did try to combine the two schools of thought.

In presenting his arguments, Socrates developed a form of reasoning called the **dialectic** or the Socratic method. He posed questions that attacked a general statement, which was assumed to be true because it was based on experience. Socrates' questions were designed to show that most responses were not adequate and did little to prove that the general statement was either true or false. The teachings of Socrates probably hindered the advance of natural science. His search for an ideal truth and his form of reasoning did not encourage the collection of facts before drawing conclusions.

Many of Socrates' ideas were adopted by his most famous student, Plato, who was both a mathematician and a philosopher. Plato used abstract theories and scorned observation in his attempts to explain the way nature worked. He also became indignant when Eudoxus, the geometer, and Archytas, another noted mathematician of the time, experimented with mechanical devices. Plato thought mechanics was a "corruption" of geometry. The study of geometry, he felt, should be purely intellectual, using measurements and equations to develop proofs.

Nevertheless, Archytas, who was Plato's friend, continued to work on mechanical inventions along with his "pure" mathematical theories. He is said to have invented the screw and the pulley. Both inventions were vital for the development of the machine industry centuries later.

Although Aristotle accepted many of Plato's teachings, his emphasis on experiments may have created a more open environment for the study of mechanics. Some historians believe it is even possible that Aristotle was one of the authors of a short work on

Socrates, the great
teacher-philosopher

mechanics. However, the mathematician Strabon, one of Aristotle's students, is most often credited with the writing. Whoever the author was, *Mechanics* is the oldest known text on engineering. It includes an attempt to explain how the lever works and also a description of gear wheels and how they move.

APPLYING MATHEMATICS

By the Hellenistic Age, which was the time following the conquests of Alexander the Great, some philosophers were openly exploring the relationship between mathematics and machinery. A few great thinkers were even willing to accept "assignments" from rulers—or more likely they gave in to the demands of kings and dictators—to design weapons and other equipment for wars.

The brilliant mathematician Archimedes designed a variety of war machines to defend the Greek city of Syracuse against Roman invaders. Archimedes was born about 287 B.C. in Syracuse on the island of Sicily and lived there most of his seventy-five years. He probably studied for a time in Alexandria and has been called one of the greatest figures in Greek mathematics and mechanics.

Some historians believe Archimedes was more a "pure" scientist than a practical one. Indeed, Archimedes himself wanted to be remembered for his work in mathematics; one of his geometrical formulas was actually engraved on his tombstone. He is remembered for making the most accurate calculation up to that time for pi (π), which is the ratio of the circumference of a circle to its diameter. Archimedes calculated pi as between $3\frac{1}{7}$ and $3\frac{10}{71}$. Today, geometry students know that pi is approximately 3.1416.

According to legend, Archimedes used lenses and mirrors to burn ships in the Roman fleet.

Plutarch, a biographer living in the second century A.D., was convinced that Archimedes looked on engineering and mechanics as "ignoble and vulgar." But as later historians have pointed out, Archimedes must have enjoyed mechanics because he invented so many machines and devices.

Early in his career, Archimedes clearly used mechanical models—he constructed movable spheres and other shapes—to work through his mathematical problems. Then he developed formulae for his proofs. He also constructed a kind of planetarium with various parts—disks and balls—that moved. The movable parts represented the sun, moon, and planets and were designed to show how these bodies moved around the earth, which was represented by a bronze ball.

MAJOR DISCOVERIES

Many legends surround Archimedes' work. One of the most widely told stories has to do with his discovery of the density of liquids. Apparently, Hieron, the king of Syracuse and Archimedes' friend, wanted to know whether his crown was made of solid gold. The king suspected that the gold had been mixed with silver, which is worth less than gold. So he asked Archimedes to try to resolve the question. The solution would have been easy if the king had allowed the crown to be melted down. Since that was not possible, Archimedes had to find another way to determine the metal content of the crown.

Archimedes supposedly discovered the answer while at a public bath. He noticed that when he got into the water, it overflowed the tub. By measuring the overflow, he found that the volume— the amount of space a thing occupies—of the spilled water was equal to the volume of his body under water. He realized he could determine the gold content of the crown by measuring the water it would displace against the amount of water displaced by a lump of gold weighing the same as the crown. The crown and lump of gold would each displace the same amount of water if the crown were solid gold. If the crown contained silver, it would displace more water, since the volume of a weight of silver is greater than the volume of the same weight of gold. With this discovery, Archimedes leaped from his bath and in his excitement raced naked down the street toward his home, shouting "EUREKA! I have found it!"

Whether the story is true or not, the point is that Achimedes was the first to develop the physical law that is now known as Archimedes' law. The law explains buoyancy, or why objects seem to lose weight in water or other liquids. This principle has been applied ever since to test precious metals.

Archimedes is especially remembered for demonstrating the principle of the lever. This hardly seems a great feat, since even the most primitive people knew how to use a heavy wooden pole or metal bar (like a crowbar) to help move a great weight. But Archimedes developed formal mathematical principles, then applied them to show that with a bar and fulcrum—or fixed support—and only a slight effort, a person could, as he put it, "move the world." He reportedly was able to singlehandedly move a loaded ship from the harbor onto the sand by applying his principle with a series of pulleys. In short, he showed how and why the principle of the lever worked, whether used on a small or large scale. Engineers apply such knowledge to this day.

One of Archimedes' most important inventions was the water screw, now known as Archimedes' screw. This seemingly simple device could bring water from a lower to a higher level. To accomplish this, Archimedes designed a helix, or spirallike pipe. As the spiral rotated inside a cylinder, it carried water upward. Archimedes' screw is still used in some developing countries where other types of pumps are not available.

MORE APPLIED SCIENCE

Following Archimedes, the ancient Greeks apparently began to slowly change their attitudes about applying science. A number of scholars studied at the school of mechanics in Alexandria. Ctesibius (teh SIB yuhs), who lived around the mid-200s B.C., was among them. Little is known about his personal life, but Ctesibius gained fame by discovering the principles of pneumatics, or the use of air movements.

How did such a discovery come about? Strange as it seems, Ctesibius learned about air movements in a barbershop! Supposedly he invented an adjustable mirror for his father, who was a barber. The mirror could be moved up and down with the use of pulleys and a lead weight. The pulley cord and the weight were inside a long tube. When the cord was pulled, the weight dropped, pushing out air as it descended and making a loud musical noise. From this phenomenon, Ctesibius gained insight into the principles of air movements, which led to such modern devices as pneumatic springs for doors.

Among Ctesibius' inventions were a new type of catapult designed to work with compressed air, a water-powered pipe organ, a force pump, and water clocks. Ctesibius' water clocks became famous, but not because they were based on a new idea. Water clocks had long been used to measure the time for specific events, such as a trial or a speech by a politician. Water was poured into a jar with a hole in the bottom, and when the jar was empty, the event ended.

Archimedes' screw brings water from one level to a higher one. It is still used today in some countries.

During antiquity, time-keeping was not measured in fractions of hours, as it is today. One-twelfth of the day was considered an hour. But that length of time changed with the seasons, since the day was measured from sunrise to sunset and days were, of course, longer in summer than in winter. So Ctesibius invented clocks able to measure time more accurately and to show hours according to the seasons.

Philon of Byzantium also seems to have studied mechanics at the Museum in Alexandria. He eventually wrote a text on pneumatics that has mostly been lost, but the fragments that remain deal primarily with the gadgets and toys that he invented.

It seems that Philon especially liked to devise "trick pitchers" with metal figures that performed acrobatics when water was poured out. Some of the cups he designed had false bottoms and "went dry" when wine or water was poured into them. He also created mechanical washbasins that operated with pulleys and weights. One of these was quite elaborate. A bronze hand held a piece of pumice stone, which was used like soap. When the user took the pumice, the hand withdrew, and enough water flowed so that a person could wash. Then the water stopped, and the hand appeared again, offering another stone.

The practice of making clever gadgets continued through the second century A.D., although Greek designers probably had more than entertainment in mind when they invented their mechanical marvels. Often these devices were used to prove that mathematical principles and theories worked.

One of the best known of the Greek "mechanical wizards" was Heron (often called Hero) of Alexandria, who perfected some of the works of Ctesibius and Philon. In his two texts *Mechanica* and *Pneumatica*, Heron described many ingenious devices similar in design to those of the earlier scientists. One delightful invention was a miniature theater with automated dancers on turntables.

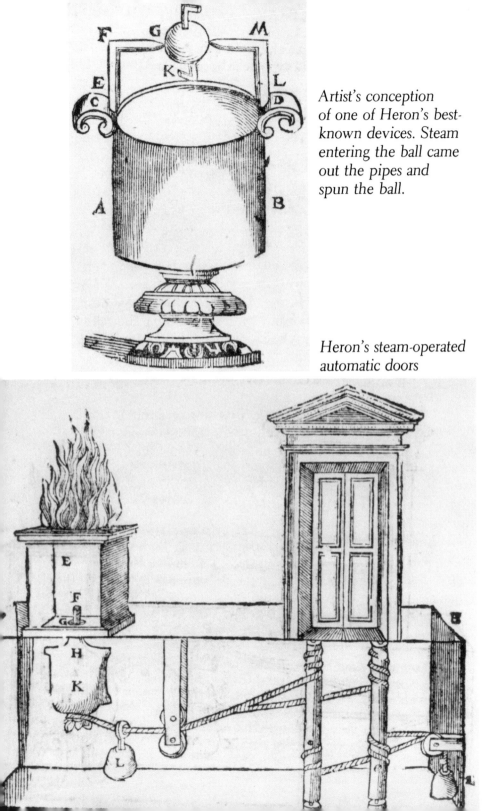

Artist's conception of one of Heron's best-known devices. Steam entering the ball came out the pipes and spun the ball.

Heron's steam-operated automatic doors

Another was a "magic pitcher," which was designed with a hole in the handle; the handle was actually a siphon. If the hole was plugged with the thumb, liquid would not pour from the pitcher.

Heron's most famous invention was a kind of toy globe that revolved by steam power. The globe was mounted on tubes that were connected to a small boiler. It was perhaps the first mechanism to use a kind of jet propulsion.

Scientist-engineers like Heron had knowledge that could have led to an earlier use of the steam engine and power-driven machinery for industry—if inexpensive cast iron had been available. But the ancient Greeks had no interest in large-scale manufacturing. The wealthy could afford to buy handmade clothing, household goods, and other needed items. Also, slave labor was used to produce much of the war equipment, many of the city buildings, and protective walls. There simply was no mass market for manufactured goods.

Yet the early Greeks developed a technology; in other words, they applied mechanical theories to produce useful goods. Along with toys and clever gadgets, Heron, for example, invented practical devices. He is known for his work in optics and for his invention of an instrument called the dioptra, which was used by surveyors to measure angles.

Other "engineers" invented such devices as mechanical computers. Evidence of this was discovered in the 1950s on the wreck of an ancient Greek ship. Some historians believe that the ancient Greeks actually accomplished a great deal in engineering and mechanics. But because of the low status given to this field of study, much of the engineering work probably was not recorded.

ENGINEERS
AND BUILDERS

Whatever the ancient Greeks' attitude toward engineering, physical and mathematical principles were certainly applied in building projects. Early Ionians adapted older Egyptian and Babylonian ideas and developed a variety of building tools, including the level and the lathe. They also invented the art of soldering. Stone-cutting and bronze-casting were other well-developed crafts of the sixth century B.C.

TEMPLES, TUNNELS,
AND STATUES

Building tools and methods were used in the construction of a huge temple at Ephesus, a Greek city on the coast of Asia Minor. The site for the temple, which was dedicated to the nature goddess Artemis, was on marshy ground. So a major problem was providing a firm foundation for the huge marble columns. How engineers came up with a successful solution is unknown, but the temple stood for hundreds of years.

One of the most remarkable Ionian building projects was an aqueduct through the base of a hill 900 feet (300 m) high. A tunnel with clay pipes carried water from a hillside spring to the city of Samos. The tunnel was over 3,000 feet (900 m) long and 6 feet (2 m) deep and wide. Clay pipes were laid in a trench 25 feet (7.6 m) deep at the bottom of the tunnel.

To build such a water conduit, crews dug from both ends and worked toward the middle of the hill. No, the two crews did not bump into each other! The tunnel was off center by 20 feet (6 m) and had to be joined at an angle. But such a close meeting was an engineering and mathematical feat. It probably required some type of surveying instruments, but no one is certain how this engineering task was accomplished.

Another great wonder of the period was the gigantic statue of the sun god, Helios. It was created by a famous sculptor Chares, who lived on the island of Rhodes. From the feet to the crown of the sun god, the statue rose 90 feet (30 m)—nearly as high as the Statue of Liberty. Such a statue, like other colossal Greek sculptures, was not only a work of art but an engineering feat as well.

The statue was constructed of stone columns, iron rods, and plates of hammered bronze riveted together. The structure was built from the ground up, so workmen apparently piled up great mounds of earth alongside, then made a pathway up to the work site. As the statue grew, so did the hill, until the sun god's crown was riveted into place. To remove the great mound, dirt had to be shoveled into baskets and carried away. The colossus was twelve years in the making, and it stood for more than five decades, finally crumbling in an earthquake in 224 B.C.

ATHENIAN BUILDERS

Massive building projects were undertaken in Athens during the 400s B.C., when Pericles, one of the world's greatest politicians, gained power as an Athenian ruler. Pericles was determined to rebuild temples and other public structures that had been destroyed in war. During the thirty years of Pericles' rule, great walls were built that extended 4 miles (over 6 km) from the city to the harbor. They protected the city from attack by sea. Pericles also called on engineers and architects to develop the harbor area and create a new port city. Hippodamus, an architect from Miletus, laid out the city with straight streets in a geometric grid pattern. Although this so-called grid plan was long known in the East, Hippodamus was the first to use such a plan in Europe. He set an example for town planning that has been used by civic engineers ever since.

The major Athenian building project was on the Acropolis, a fortified, rocky area overlooking the city. A pathway lined with statues led to the Acropolis, where marble temples and shrines were built. The most magnificent temple was the Parthenon with its splendid columns. Inside was a towering gold and ivory statue of the goddess Athena. Another statue of Athena, cast in bronze, stood outside the Parthenon and loomed nearly 60 feet (18 m) high over the city so that it could be seen, sparkling in the sun, from ships far out on the sea. The bronze figure has disappeared, but ruins of the Parthenon attract thousands of visitors each year, and its remaining columns are still awesome to behold.

During the time of Pericles drama flourished in Athens, and open-air theater structures were carved into rocky hillsides. These curved theaters with tiered rock benches and a great circular stage area below became well known for their acoustics. Architects understood the nature of sound waves and designed the hillside theaters so that even a whisper on stage could be heard by people in the top decks. Theaters also included advanced stage machinery, such as movable scenery and hoists that lowered actors, who played the parts of gods, onto the stage.

The building projects in Athens came to an end when war

The Parthenon, perched atop the Acropolis

broke out with Sparta, a small city-state in the southern Peloponnesus. The Greeks did not build again on a grand scale until the next century, during the time of Alexander the Great.

ALEXANDRIA AND PHAROS

Alexandria, the thriving Greek city established by Alexander in Egypt, was built in about 322 B.C. on a narrow strip of land between the Mediterranean Sea and a lake that fed into the Nile River. Alexander commissioned Dinocrates, from the island of Rhodes, to plan and supervise the construction of the city. Dinocrates was the most prominent Greek architect of his time, known in particular for designing the temple in Ephesus.

The city of Alexandria was designed around two major arteries. Canopic, the main avenue, ran straight through the city for 3 miles (5 km) and was 100 feet (30 m) wide. Another shorter avenue was perpendicular to Canopic, bisecting it. The crossing marked the city's center. All other streets were laid out parallel to the main avenues.

Along with homes, there were many public buildings, including marble palaces and temples, huge stadia, and the great educational center, the Museum. Several parks provided green space. A great canal was dug to connect Alexandria with a branch of the heavily traveled Nile River, and two harbors offered access to the sea.

The main sea harbor was opposite an island called Pharos that was joined to the city by a breakwater, or dike. Not only did the island act as a protective buffer for the harbor, it was also the site for a gigantic lighthouse, one of the Seven Wonders of the World. A marvel of engineering, it was built after Alexander's death in the mid-200s B.C. Sailors who were guided by the skyscraper christened it Pharos, after the island, and the lighthouse was known by that name until the fourteenth century A.D., when it was destroyed by an earthquake.

A spectacular structure, Pharos rose over 400 feet (120 m). It was built upon a heavy stone platform in three sections. The lower section was square, the middle section was shaped like an octagon (eight-sided figure), and the top section was a tall cylinder. Stone ramps and stairways connected the sections. Centuries later, travelers who saw the lighthouse said the stones were "united by molten lead," so tightly joined that Pharos remained solid, even "though the surge of the sea from the north incessantly beats against the structure." At the top of the lighthouse, a torch burned day and night as a beacon for navigators.

SHIPBUILDING

Huge merchant ships, elaborately painted and adorned with ivory and gold figures, were also built during the third century B.C. The ships carried thousands of tons of grain, fish, wool, and other freight between Greek cities and other trade centers in Europe and Asia. Large crews manned the ships, including hundreds of rowers. One ship was said to have been equipped with huge oars with lead handles, making the oars very heavy but easy to use because they were so well balanced.

Hieron, one of the Greek rulers of Syracuse on the southeast coast of Sicily, built a fleet of ships to transport wheat, a major crop on the island. One of those wheat transports was called *Lady of Syracuse* and apparently was designed to be a combination freighter, warship, and royal yacht. It was built with three masts, perhaps the first of its kind in the world. The ship's timbers were covered with strips of linen canvas and then with pitch (tar). Over that was a sheath of lead tiles. Heavy bronze rivets held the ship parts together.

This mosaic depicts a Greek ship near the Pharos lighthouse,
one of the Seven Wonders of the World.

The interior of *Lady of Syracuse* held not only wheat cargo but also horses, a fish tank, a water tank, and containers for wood, ovens, and other cooking equipment. According to a description written in the third century B.C., quarters for the ruler Hieron and other officials were large enough to "hold fifteen couches and contained three apartments." The royal quarters had a "flooring made of a variety of stones, in the pattern of which was wonderfully wrought the entire story of the *Iliad*; also in the furniture, the ceiling, and the doors all these themes were artfully represented." The ship also contained a gymnasium, promenades (walkways) with plants and flowers, a lavish shrine to the goddess Aphrodite, a library "large enough for five couches," and a bathroom "of three-couch size" with bronze tubs and marble wash basins. The crew for such a luxurious ship numbered in the thousands. In addition, it was heavily armed, since pirate attacks were common on the Mediterranean Sea.

ADVANCES IN ENGINEERING

In ancient Greece, massive construction of any kind depended on a variety of engineering techniques. Many techniques were improved, such as the cranes developed to lift great weights. Builders began to use block and tackle with pulleys operated by a tread-wheel. To work the treadwheel, five or six men walked inside a cagelike drum, thus turning the wheel that pulled the ropes of the hoist.

The design of water wheels also progressed with an invention by Philon, who created so many mechanical gadgets. He is said to have invented a device in which buckets on a chain, driven by a water wheel, brought water up from a stream to the top of a well-like structure. A later mechanism, based on the same concept, was used in grain mills.

Although the influence of ancient Greek technicians—engineers and mechanics—was not as great as that of the "pure" scientists, the technology was a foundation for later developments. With the use of water power, for example, the early Greeks showed that nature's energy could be concentrated. Running water could be used instead of human or animal power to accomplish certain tasks. From the time of ancient Greece to this day, there has been steady progress in the technology that harnesses natural forces—from water and wind to nuclear power—to work for people.

THE HERITAGE
OF THE
ANCIENT GREEKS

Greek ideas and ways of life spread far and wide, especially during the Hellenistic Age. But over the centuries, wars between city-states and empires took their toll. Greek power diminished and was eventually destroyed. A long war between Carthage and Rome ended with a victory for the Romans in 146 B.C. As a result, the Greek mainland became part of the Roman empire. During the next century, other Greek territories in Asia were taken over by the Romans.

Yet Greek ideas and accomplishments did not die. The Romans were greatly influenced by the vast treasury of Greek knowledge. Unlike the Greeks, the Romans were eager to apply science; they used physical principles developed by Greek scientists to build walls, roads, aqueducts, stadia, harbors, and many other public facilities. Although the Romans did little to advance "pure" science, they passed on Greek learning by absorbing and adapting it. As the Roman Empire expanded, Hellenistic culture also spread. The Greek legacy even survived the fall of the Roman Empire centuries later, as scholars in the Arab-speaking world revived the process of collecting and analyzing scientific material and passing it on to Western Europe.

Today, the influence of ancient Greece is evident in many disciplines. From inquiries into the nature of the universe to the development of amusing gadgets and useful mechanisms, the work of Greek scientists has had an effect on many aspects of modern life. The Greek scientific contributions are many, and only a few have been described on these pages. But the accomplishments are worth repeating in summary.

Modern medicine owes much to Greek physicians who passed on an ethical code and tried to keep medical practices free of superstition and mythical "cures." Greek scholars laid the foundations for advanced geometry, trigonometry, and calculus, for theories of organic evolution, and for organizing and classifying information. Philosopher-scientists from Thales onward should be remembered especially for their part in developing ways to explain the workings of nature in such disciplines as anatomy, biology, botany, astronomy, and geography.

The scientific world has the early Greek philosophers to thank for developing methods of reasoning and research practices. They also transmitted their love of learning, a respect for wisdom, and an understanding of the need to be diligent in the search for truth. These qualities are accepted today as valuable assets.

Perhaps the most important contribution to science is the Greek gift for rational inquiry. It is an essential tool for research and continued progress in technology; it may even help in the struggle to find some peaceful method for resolving conflicts between the divergent peoples of the world.

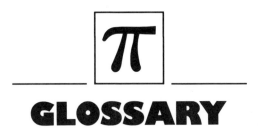

GLOSSARY

cosmos—an orderly universe

deductive reasoning—drawing conclusions by reasoning from a general law to a specific case

dialectic—logical discussion

eclipse—a total or partial blocking of light that passes from one heavenly body to another

gnomon—the pointer on a sundial that creates a shadow to indicate the time of day

humors—body fluids

inductive reasoning—making generalizations from specific facts

papyrus—a grass-like plant

syllogism—a form of reasoning in which a logical conclusion is drawn from premises

π

FOR FURTHER READING

Arnott, Peter D. *An Introduction to the Greek World.* New York: St. Martin's Press, 1967.

Asimov, Isaac. *The Greeks: A Great Adventure.* Boston: Houghton Mifflin, 1965.

Bernal, J.D. *Science in History, Vol. I: The Emergence of Science.* Cambridge, Mass.: The MIT Press, 1971.

Bowra, C.M. *The Greek Experience.* Cleveland and New York: World, 1957.

Bowra, C.M., and Editors of Time-Life Books. *Great Ages of Man: Classical Greece.* New York: Time, 1965.

Brumbaugh, Robert. *Ancient Greek Gadgets and Machines.* New York: Crowell, 1966.

Crow, John A. *Greece: The Magic Spring.* New York: Harper & Row, 1970.

DeCamp, L. Sprague. *The Ancient Engineers.* Garden City, New York: Doubleday, 1963.

Durant, Will. *The Story of Civilization: Life of Greece.* New York: Simon & Schuster, 1939.

Editors of Readers Digest Association. *The Last Two Million Years.* London and New York: Readers Digest, 1973-1974.

Finley, M.I. *The Ancient Greeks: An Introduction to Their Life and Thought.* New York: Viking, 1963.

Goldstein, Thomas. *Dawn of Modern Science: From the Arabs to Leonardo Da Vinci.* Chapter 2, "Ancient Roots." Boston: Houghton Mifflin, 1980.

Hooper, Finley. *Greek Realities: Life and Thought in Ancient Greece.* New York: Scribner's, 1967.

Kitto, H.D.F. *The Greeks.* Chicago: Aldine Publishing Company, 1964. (First published by Penguin Books Ltd., 1951).

Miller, Helen Hill. *Greek Horizons.* New York: Scribner's, 1961.

Murdoch, John E. *Album of Science: Antiquity and the Middle Ages.* New York: Scribner's, 1984.

Ronan, Colin A. *Science: Its History and Development Among the World's Cultures.* New York: Facts on File, 1983.

Schwartz, George, and Philip Bishop, eds. *Moments of Discovery.* New York: Basic Books, 1958.

Singer, Charles. *A Short History of Scientific Ideas to 1900.* New York: Oxford University Press, 1959.

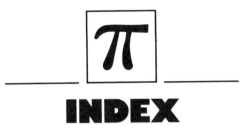

INDEX

ABOUT THE AUTHOR

Kathlyn Gay is the author of numerous books, magazine articles, and plays for both young readers and adults. Her book *Acid Rain*, published by Franklin Watts, was cited by both the National Council of Social Studies and the National Science Teachers Association as one of the notable children's books for 1983. *Crisis in Education*, another of her Watts books, was selected by the National Education Association as "one of the most important recent publications in education" in 1987. She and her husband, Arthur L. Gay, live in Elkhart, Indiana.